Shell

For Brian

from Ian

With Best Wishes

Mexborough

19th June, 2007

Shell Island

Ian Parks

Ian Parks

WAYWISER

First published in 2006 by

THE WAYWISER PRESS

9 Woodstock Road, London N4 3ET, UK
P.O. Box 6205, Baltimore, MD 21206, USA
www.waywiser-press.com

Managing Editor
Philip Hoy

Associate Editors
Joseph Harrison   Clive Watkins   Greg Williamson

A CIP catalogue record for this book is available from the British Library

ISBN-10: 1-904130-19-4
ISBN-13: 978-1-904130-19-2

Printed and bound by
Cromwell Press Ltd., Trowbridge, Wiltshire

For Betty and Judd

Acknowledgements

"The Guest" and "Goldenrod" appeared in *Poetry* (Chicago).

"The Western Sea" appeared in *The Observer.*

"The Catch" appeared in *The Express.*

"Jazz Train" appeared in *Paging Doctor Jazz: A Verse Anthology* (Shoestring Press).

"The Great Divide", "Shell Island", "Jazz Train", "White Horse", "Songs of Freedom", and "Comrade" were included in *The Great Refusal* (Flux Gallery Press).

Navigation Road was featured in a poster and postcard project by Time to Read (Manchester Libraries).

Narrow Boat was featured in a poster project by Hospital Arts for North East Yorkshire.

"A Valley Affair", "Shell Island" and "Lavernock" were included on a CD recording, *The Angel of the North* (Tarantula).

Other poems appeared in the following magazines: *Aesthetica, Acumen, Agenda, Brando's Hat, Chiron Review* (USA), *Connections, Dream Catcher, English* (Journal of the English Association), *Interchange, The Liberal, Magma, Oxford Today, Pearl* (USA), *Pennine Platform, Poetry Daily* (USA), *Poetry File, Poetry Greece, Poetry Review, Poetry Scotland, The Reader, The Reater, The Rialto, The Slab, West 47* (Republic of Ireland), *The Wide Skirt, The Yellow Crane.*

The author would like to thank the Royal Literary Fund, the Society of Authors, the John Downes/Oppenheim Trust, Leeds Philosophical and Literary Society, and Hawthornden Castle International Retreat for Writers for providing assistance during the writing of this collection.

The author would also like to thank Clive Watkins, his editor at Waywiser, for many helpful suggestions.

The following poems carry dedications: "A Greek Epiphany" for Ian Pople, "Comrade" for Milner Place, "Narrow Boat" for Andrew Oldham, "The Anarchists" for Ed Reiss, "The Loneliness of Men in Midnight Bars" for Peter Knaggs, "At the Water's Edge" for William Park, "New England Afternoon" for Jules Smith, "East River" for T.F. Griffin, "Encounter at the Well" for Tony Flynn, "Jazz Train" for Peter Lewin.

Contents

Contents

Goldenrod

If I don't say it, someone will:
the wind blows through the goldenrod
as death flows through a crowd.
I watch it from a distance:
the whole field lifts and stirs.
Close up, it holds the promise
of a less than perfect world.
I knew the thing before I knew its name.
Now all I know is what the name implies:
a life of pure sensation
or the rod some angel brings
announcing a momentous death or birth,
each face expectant, brightly-lit.
I say the name and what it means
until the meaning blurs.
The wind blows through the goldenrod
as death flows through a crowd.
Nothing is accomplished,
and the world is changed by it.

Shell Island

The girl is tall
and never thinks of food
unless he brings her
oysters from the bay
arranged with lemon
on an oval plate.

It is their only
luxury. At night
an oil-lamp swings
above the bed;
a tarnished mirror glints
across the hall;

their furniture is sanded
to a cool, transparent sheen.
Incomers, they begin
to feel at home.
Their new republic
is a state of mind

in which the world
of commerce lays no claim.
It has its laws,
its languages – a grove
of olives where
the freed bird sings.

The shells of all
the oceans gather here:
a cache of pink
exotic coils banked up
against the winter tide.
I ask if it's still possible,

this pool of dreams
and solitudes
in which the driftwood
floats at rest
and lives retract,
becoming simplified.

Across the bay
the new refinery
lights up their hemisphere;
a still white centre
pulses and dilates.
Complex, entire,

it holds their studied
gaze: as alien, cold
and insecure
as the force it draws
its power from,
the city it anticipates.

The Sandbank

I could take you to the sandbank
    where my father dug for bait,
        turning his shadow over

with a spade. I could find
    the exact meaning of his words,
        the lost configuration

as he stooped to lift the worms
    while a red sun edged its circuit
        round the world. A silence

fell between us as he worked,
    slicing the slabs to wetness
        at my feet. A million grains

have come and gone and still
    the sandbank keeps its shape,
        a forked stream into which

the memory bleeds.
    My father's shadow holds
        the ridge: it moves when I move,

waves and I wave back, blocks out
    the sunlight where I saw it last
        and when I draw near, recedes.

Kite

We're braced against the wind, my son and I, out in the open
where the blue begins. Over the fence our comprehension ends,
the sea-gust lifting gulls into a clear and cloudless sky.
All that he is or has been up to now is concentrated
in his upturned eyes, his hands that tug the tightening strings.
The kite we bought him, twice his size,
dips, veers and falters out towards the edge. He takes a breath,
then races after it. And I'm reminded of three things –

distinct, interconnected – that come from somewhere
deep inside: the child who lost his footing on these cliffs,
left only a scream where his laughing face had been;
the man whose kite had lifted him above the rooftops,
the shifting estuary, then dropped him safely on the other side
who said he loved the looking down, the thrill, the slow descent;
and Icarus with arms spread wide, his face a mask
of pure astonishment, the hot wax dripping from his wings.

White Horse

More welcoming than any hand or eye,
the white horse browsing in a field
of meadowsweet and rue. My curtains opened

on a world unmade: the fruit not taken
and the word unsaid. At night I watched
as dark gave it a shape – a thing of two dimensions

scooped and levelled on the hill, put there
to commemorate some great and lost event
that mattered when it happened but has no meaning now,

a sacred image we can't understand.
By day it was the thing it was again, breathing hotly,
nodding at the fence, flicking flies off with its tail,

thinking of nothing as I passed it at the gate.
What does a horse dream as it stands there in the haze?
I know it gave a meaning to my summer in the place

and to my own forgetting – half what it was
and half what it became – emblematic, lost in shade,
a liquid eye unblinking as it took grass from my hand.

A Valley Affair

A silent girl with auburn hair
moved in the cottage opposite.

Between us there was nothing
but the valley's steep incline,

the window where she used to sit
as winter turned to spring.

She lived in rumours heard
around the town: a broken marriage,

bruises, kids; a midnight
crossing, then the trek

along that wild peninsula
to here – a slate-and-granite cottage

with a sloping roof,
blocking the tangled entrance

to a disused copper mine.
At night a single candle

drew my gaze, turning
her body over in my dreams.

I knew we shared a birth-sign
when she came, asking for water

at a neighbour's farm
and watched her white legs flexing

as she started up the hill,
a transparent plastic canister

slung over one bare arm,
needing both to help and look

as if each impulse were the same.
What made me hesitate?

But hesitate I did – until
the year's first crocus

nudged the soil. Then I was
running, making for

that crumbling whitewashed cottage
behind its drystone wall – and found

what you expected me to find:
cold ash flaking in the grate,

a rolling bottle, mattress, rugs,
an absent presence

filling out the place, the latch
still ticking on her gate.

The Guest

He came from nowhere, unannounced;
    ate up the olives, drank the wine,
made love to the teenage daughter
    with the window open wide
as a gold fan sliced the air

above the bed; spent languid evenings
    on their balcony under the shade
of orange trees, indifferent to the view
    across a drunken city to the white acropolis
which rose above exhaust fumes, shimmering heat.

All the cheques he gave them bounced.
    He taught the younger brother how to steal.
Small acquisitions from the marketplace
    appeared whenever he came home: a naked Aphrodite,
perfumed oils, a book of love poems,

silken handkerchiefs. The eldest son
    was taken for a ride. A postcard came
from Piraeus. He won't be coming back.
    Unquestioned, uninvited, an identity in doubt,
he showed the woman how it feels

to enter the live current of the street
    at midnight as her husband fell asleep
and dreamt of things you only see
    in shadows on an ancient frieze.
When they came down one morning, he was gone,

left nothing but a secret sign
    in wine stains on the table top.
He was making for the islands and the deep
    Aegean blue, walked barefoot on the quayside
with the wings behind his heels.

A Greek Epiphany

Think of a golden crucifix
    suspended as it falls;
        then think of how the cold waves

haul it down. The priest
    stands empty-handed on the shore:
        his eyes might catch

the wide arc it describes
    before it strikes the water,
        glints and sinks. For him

it is a necessary loss. The crowd
    massed on the harbour
        have no reason to believe:

they're still, expectant,
    waiting for a sign –
        except no sign is given

but these poor, half-naked boys
    who dive through swathes
        of sunlight to retrieve

a blessing for the living
    and the dead, extracting
        meaning from the sea –

its monuments of white
    and fallen stone, its dark
        unruffled bed.

Edward Hopper and the Lighthouse

The dim interiors he's famous for
give way to this: a stretch of empty coastline,
sandbanks, dunes, a lone gull
scudding through unclouded skies.

The city held him captive: in its grip
he peered through hotel windows
and reported what he saw: a woman
smoothing out her wrinkled seams,

diners, drug-stores, lobbies, neon signs.
Now everything has opened out
except the shuttered lighthouse which he sees
as if for the first time, as if its posture

and its clear, uncluttered lines
had somehow freed it from his troubled dreams.
He's testing the perspective of new doubt,
looking at the world through half-closed eyes.

Comrade

He came to a place of clear water, some distance
from the harbour and its noise. The chapel door was open;
he shrugged and stepped inside. She draped her promise

like a purple robe across the altar where he paused
to take in what was offered by pale sunlight as it came
against the glass. The incense made him hesitate.

His journey was a long one: as he slipped from port to port
the ache that he called memory began to play him false,
hauling past and future into one uncertain tense

of heat and water, dangerous afternoons, high passes
through the mountains, that gathered to the lost word *Spain*.
He was a traveller after all, accustomed to the strangeness

of an unfamiliar bed: worn sheets and love poems improvised
from nothing but a snatch of gypsy song – a salt taste recollected
in old age and under the cold stars. What circumstances

made him disregard the cities with their twisted minarets,
their cautious guards with arm bands and the market squares
where everything – the bangles, carpets, women – had a price

but still had to be bargained for, relinquishing the pull
of perfume and sleek bodies for a life among the altitudes
where air came thin and precious and the peasants

scraped a living from the soil? Nothing was forgotten:
red flags against a ragged dawn, torn posters flapping free,
the headlines, broadcasts, barricades, dead comrades

fallen under olive trees – all were subsumed into the shifting core
he called himself; blurred nights, hung-over mornings
when the sun stood white and fragile as the moon,

a hot flamenco racing through his head. Home had been
an exile after this: the sameness of the mining towns,
the greyness of the landscape and the flatness of the beer.

Those bars, cantinas, dark saloons had taken from him
but they also gave. He knew all there was to know
of victory and loss, having tasted both and found them

much the same. And now this god had failed him too:
they nailed his message to an empty cross or kept it locked
in jewelled reliquaries under the altar, out of sight.

What hidden impulse made him turn into a mountain track,
decide it was as good a place as any to set down
and make an end where air was scarce as water

and bats, erratic in the moonlight, veer and flit?
We carried out his final wish, brought back the body,
buried him at sea, threw garlands as it drifted to the bed.

Someone discovered his forgotten poems and read them
as we turned to face the shore. They spoke to us
from under the cold waves of love and its stark opposite.

Seahorses

As I remember, you start to forget
the long road leading nowhere
except back, the Cretan fisherman
who emptied out his net
onto the quayside smiling
his toothless, pleading smile,
imploring us to buy and eat
the live catch flapping hopeless
on the slab.

As you remember,
I start to forget the afternoon
you left me in the shade to dive
among the rock-pools, half-submerged –
and wanting love to last
a little longer than we said it would,
encountering a shoal of them
as they came wafting past,
disturbing the warm current
as they went: spiked back,
ribbed spine, coiled tail
and lowered head.

What we both agree on
are the seahorse souvenirs
strung out along the shop-fronts,
turning brittle in the heat;
and you not touching, holding back,
keeping to the shadows like a child
who'd met them in their element
and couldn't bear to look upon them dead.

The Mirrored Room

The airmen etched their names
and the names of their new lovers
with penknives in the bright
reflective glass. We traced
their fragile lettering
as darkness spread outside.

It was your city after all:
its overrated skyline
cutting shapes into the dark,
the river threading solitude
through regions of the heart.

Whoever stands there,
turning to the light, discovers
how they went from here
to death above the Channel,
France or Germany,
leaving a scratched reminder in the place.

I don't know what it meant to you
but what it meant for me
was sudden recognition:
of how love looks
when circumstance
has stripped it cold and bare
and how those random pairings
made tenable by war
were overlaid across your searching eyes,
rewritten in your raised, enquiring face.

The Catch

When my father married,
he gave up fishing for good
and sold his rod and line
to buy the marriage bed.
But his dreams are haunted still
by damp river-banks and mist
where he stoops to dip a net,
lifting the catch from memory
in a rehearsal of regret.
The reel unwinds inside his head.

East River

You might wake up at midnight and decide
   to go down to the cold east river,
   to watch the big ships roll in on the tide
and listen to the blues. The man who plays it

makes no compromise: he knows
   which notes to hold and which to hide
   and how a certain atmosphere can cling
around the melting chord of a lost song.

I go there when there's nothing to discover,
   when the question and the answer
   sound the same. The estuary narrows
to a blade of silver light

becoming somewhere all the things we dream –
   an undercurrent drifting deep and slow
   past wharves and piers and dockside bars
where lovers, poets, lunatics and all the drowned men go

to catch the falling beat and improvise.
   I go there when the tides have come together
   and the waters start to rise,
for the love of what is silent, has no aim and runs forever.

Skating at Somerset House

Pavilion lights – a hazy blend
of purple, amber, blue –
smooth out the oval rink

and make it shine.
Stacked and shelved and classified
the dead have lost

all interest in the snow
and how the living move through it
as if they've been transformed,

The living too
have learned to look away:
they skim the frost

and never stop to think
a razor's edge
divides them from the dead

who press cold faces
up against the glass. A helix
like a thread connects them all.

They watch their own reflection
in the ice – the married couples
and their kids made one

in concentration as they pass,
shouting to the frozen stars
and trying not to fall.

Narrow Boat

There must be other sunsets
like the sunset I've just seen,

another way of knowing
what I knew as darkness fell –

what needed words
before it could be known.

The boat might be the cause of it –
that or the smooth canal

that slides under the bridges
without discourse or restraint.

Whichever is responsible
I neither touch nor name.

A trace of oil
floats on the waiting lock;

the furthest reaches slip from view,
lost in a bank of weeds.

Moored here beside the towpath
in the first cool summer rain

something unsaid
has come into its own.

Etched in Glass

Four years now – or is it five? –
I slept in an attic bedroom
with an unexpected view

of slanting rooftops, terracotta tiles,
where a lone gull blinked
on a chimney-pot

and the sea was white for miles.
A tinted window limited
the little left to see.

How do we connect
with what we were unless
some image roots us

to the source, delineates the selves
through which we pass?
For me it is a square

of greenish light, a skewered heart
and under it the names
of two dead lovers etched in glass.

The Storm

The night before your father died
    you struggled with the storm.
        It came against you with the force
    of something understood,
distressing cattle in the yard

and grappling with your dress.
    It scoured the narrow valley,
        ripping trees up by the roots.
    All night the dogs were restless;
geese raised white and futile wings

as if to fend off death.
    When they broke the news to you,
        the storm had run its course –
    one of those perfect northern dawns,
the wrecked transmitter scattered

over uplands streaked with mist.
    Your voice came cracked and thin
        over the wires. By midnight
    I was there – your cramped,
haphazard farmhouse flanked by moors.

I took a candle up the narrow stairs;
    shadows flailed around your head.
        Then in the empty kitchen I sat down
    to one spare meal of bread and bitter herbs,
drank wine from your dark cellar,

furred with cold, and tasted there
    for the first time, among the stripped
        essentials of a life I leave and enter
    at my will, a grief so huge and inexplicable
that breaks and won't be comforted.

The Anarchists

It's late. The sun refuses
to go down. And still they sit
above the empty square,
adrift on the smoke
of cheap cigars. One leans
forward, cracks a joke;
another tastes the sweet
deliberate air that swims up

from the city street
where girls are selling roses
to the guilty bourgeoisie.
Assassins, they repudiate
the simple sabotage.
Instead the system crumbles
piece by piece, infected
by the ludicrous desire

at large in the heart
of this lost metropolis.
The lie is in the absinthe
with its green and deadly stare.
In dim cafés
and in the shuddering park
new loves betray
each other with a kiss.

China Blue

I'm working on the border, sifting through
the debris of a dozen shattered lives.
Everything I touch falls back to dust
or comes to pieces in my hands
except this twist of porcelain and here,
three yards apart, two blue-veined fragments

that might still connect despite the silt
and slippage in between. Is it a mapping
of the human heart, this frail unfinished narrative
in which two lovers make their way
across an ornamental bridge pursued
by someone's father and the world not noticing?

I scrape away the years of mud. Her parasol
still tilts into the light. Her arm still links
with his as they step into the blue;
a squat pagoda sits out on the lake
in the centre on an island hung with trees.
Two love birds flutter off towards the rim.

Bronze Horses

Bought as a pair because I couldn't choose
between the stallion and the mare,
they stand in opposition on the shelf.
Something in the way he turns to her

implies acceptance of a sort
although one came from Athens, one from Rome,
and several generations separate
his hard cold stare from hers. Stiff-necked,

green-tinted, all energy contained,
he looks across the space between
and tries to make it work. Her argument
is fashioned in her limbs – her arched back

aching for release – who always knew
to be is to explore. I see them and forget them,
subsumed into the shadow on the wall,
poised at either end of the same thought.

End of Season

The swimming pool flakes dry aquamarine.
Here women who have loved and lost
find consolation in the winter tide

returning summer debris to the shore.
We think we overhear them when they say,
This is my limit and my resting place –

a backwater town that backs onto the sea
where I can question my identity
until the day I die. In threadbare bars,

in station waiting rooms, this sense of absence
coming back to me: the shutters are down,
the lights have gone out, our sheets smell of the sea.

Songs of Freedom

And yes, I will be waiting where the road
dips suddenly, but not this side of winter
and not where you're expecting me to be.
Come north this time and find me when it's done,
my forehead pressed against the flashing dome,

my hair cropped short just as it used to be,
and tell me how the landscape looks
from your side of the bay. Does it retain
its dark complexity where moored boats tilt
and nothing stays the same?

These freedom songs are molten to the core:
they rise from empty workings, gantries, wharves –
unguarded moments where a thought might grow.
So when they sing them what I hear
are voices of lost workers as they echo underground;

and when I hear them what I see
are miles of rail track, cuttings, seams,
vast waterways and networks heaving up
to reach the light. This place might claim me yet:
its cold, its sharp austerities, its sense

of having nothing left to prove –
which finds me in the back streets
of a hard backwater town, feeding the darkness
with the dispossessed, the words of our dead language
stuck and spinning in the groove.

Peninsula

A cold day, a clear day
and a fresh wind blowing
inland from the sea. Each mile

involves a new discovery
as hills slope into barrows
and the near horizon

opens suddenly with a rim of blue
and these black-headed gulls
imploring and debating

over this disputed ground.
The island, domed and silent,
holds its course. And you

old poet, waiting at the end –
your house a mound
of weathered stones, your bed a pile

of sticks – do you reduce
the given word to signs
and portents no-one understands?

Or is it that I make my way
to you across this stretch
of ever-tapering land

to mirror my own longing
for the city you reject
by being here? Almost there

I catch the drift of anonymity:
the land-mass narrows
and the heart responds.

Navigation Road

An unexpected halt:
and part of me
was five miles down the track,
lost to the thought
of how it felt
to wake up in your arms.
Pale sunlight seeped
across the sloping roofs
of another undistinguished
northern town – red-brick,
forgettable – that only
made it to the map
because the lines converge.
Mist cleared from the canal.
A schoolgirl boarded, dropped her book,
and left it where it fell.
From now expect
a slight shift of the heart.
Our hands are linked
under these winter sheets;
our tracks are running parallel.

Promises and Smiles

We live under a government
of promises and smiles.

Out here you wouldn't know it:
the pit-heads are grassed over,

ice cracks the frozen lake
and under last night's sealing frost

the hills are clear for miles.
The city where I leave you

bears the weight: it groans
under a winter sky

these bright new stars transfix
where every hoarding shows a face

and each converted loft contains
a hive of millionaires.

Is this where the heart
and commerce meet —

in a loose affiliation
of our little love affairs

with what is gained and what is lost?
Redress these beggars

in the mindless street —
the rule of love and politics.

The Loneliness of Men in Midnight Bars

Avoiding contact with the barmaid's eye
is what they do when closing time arrives.
Washed up here on the reaches
of this tired northern shore
they learn the details of each other's lives,
sink back into the worn upholstery

and dream. The city has forgotten
its proud past: how once
it closed its gates and barred its doors
against a king demanding arms
to punish parliament. In rooms like this
men hunched into conspiracies,

planned revolutions, tried to stand alone.
It's too late now to start the day again,
and so we take the sidestreet,
wander in, move under lamplight,
voluble and free. They see us
and their faces turn to stone.

Window Seat

There's complicity in this:
the way the landscape

curves itself around
the huge bay window

where you come to sit
each morning before dawn.

What wakes you isn't birdsong
or the need to be alone;

not frost releasing
its impoverished hold

out in the orchard
where the dead tree bends –

but silence with its shades
and undertones

that mesh their textures
through the vacant glass,

making new patterns
in the empty frame:

a secret in the waiting –
and the waiting never ends.

Balthus and His Model in Early Evening Light

My only interest is the pose: legs parted,
fingers interlocked behind the head.
So as I sketch, I merely guess
what thoughts produce the half-derisive scowl
which spreads across your upturned face.
You think my purpose is to slip
a careless hand between the folds
of your unbuttoned shirt, caress
into pure tenderness the small breasts
rising there. *And if you did I'd choose not to resist.*
Quite soon you'll watch me hesitate,

then roll white stockings back below scuffed knees,
smooth down the pleated skirt you made me hitch
above my naked thighs. The fire collapses
into its own dream. The Paris streets are lit.
Like you I might have loved them once.
Why do you paint me dressed for school?
And then, when all your work is done,
what makes you stand back from the frame,
gaze at the canvas – not at me –
as if the softness gathering there
had hardened into innocence?

Anderby Creek

I went east by south-east
to the place, found everything
was there just as they'd said:
the one road leading out

and leading in: an empty beach-house,
brittle dunes, a few groynes
sloping down into the sea.
No one I met there knew my name.

The creek was an invention:
all I saw were dykes and streams,
a pumping station churning
night and day. I couldn't buy

a razor or a pen; the coffee pot
poured sand grains from its spout;
the only pub was closed.
At night I lit a candle

and looked out; a blank sky
pressed against the empty frame
where nothing was reflected
but my face. I couldn't get

a signal on my phone. Next morning
I resolved to try again.
The road was blocked with drifts
of blown-back sand. I walked down

to the shoreline in a mist
and tried to find the reason why I came.
Something had edged me closer
to the brink, dissolving my identity

in sea and sand and air.
As for the place, it really does exist
between the flatlands and the tide.
Look on the map; you'll find it there.

At the Water's Edge

This morning I began
   the long haul back,
woke to the scent
   of floorboards sanded down,

shook off the lingering doubt
   of last night's dream,
then turned to face the sea.
   Blue paint was flaking

from the weathered porch;
   a current, a deep stream
was running underneath,
   unsettling the calm weather

with a reason of its own,
   dividing what things are
from what they seem,
   inviting me to take

the three steps down, to cross
   a stretch of streaked
and hard-ribbed sand
   to where a narrow strip,

a ragged spur, intruded
   as a thought intrudes
across the mind's scoured floor –
   reformed, reshaped, impossible

to map, except at midnight
   and in dreams. From there
I looked back at the stranded house –
   not a house, really,

but a wooden shack
    thrown up one weekend, improvised
from scraps of nothing
    drifted on the beach:

some planks, a spar, black pitch
    and clouded glass;
so fragile that a gale
    might send it back

to its unconstituted state.
    The shoreline was exhausted.
It was as if I'd said
    to someone at my side –

someone I'd loved once
    in a place like this,
a place of indecision
    where things form and fall apart –

I'm going now. It's for the best
    you watch me disappear
into this watercolour
    drained of light

and don't come looking for me
    when I'm gone. That's when I saw her
at the water's edge,
    drawing the string

of an imaginary bow,
    flexing her concentration
in the moment of the act,
    making an arc of nothing

which she held
    and then released.
I was an interloper
    on a timeless scene,

made almost guilty
    by her almost-nakedness,
not knowing if the looking
    was what made the wave collapse.

Tonight I take a candle
    through the place,
discover it by touch,
    wade through it

like a lost empiricist
    who only knows for sure
the things he hears or sees
    as Zeno's arrow

flies into the dark.
    Flying fast, it occupies
a space forever equal
    to its always-equal size.

Aimed at the centre
    of an endless flight
it holds its course
    and never hits the mark.

The Ice Hotel

The women, too, they say, are made of ice,
except you touch them and they fail to melt.
A waiter brings them cocktails on a clear
    and icy tray; guests sleep together on an icy bed.

And here it's always winter. You arrive
hauled in by huskies over white terrain
to enter an iced lobby vaulted like a polar cave;
    your fingers tingle as you sign your name.

This is where association ends
and all distinctions fade, where you can watch
the Northern Lights perform their nimble dance
    across an empty sky. Executives

would never venture here – a place of light
and mirrors, glass façades – where the time
is always midnight and the tense is always now.
    Deep down below vast oceans move; poets and their lovers

come to breathe the sterile air, look out across
the frozen miles and dream of nothingness. A cold sun shines,
and every year they come with picks and saws
    to scour the ice and build it all again.

Ghost

Slowly your touch fades from me.
Again I'm only dreaming,
but the soft curve of your spine

has left its indentation
on the sheet, a question mark
no answer satisfies.

What constitutes a haunting?
Is it a chill encounter
at the bottom of the stair –

an unclenched fist, a rapid movement
in the dark, dispelling air?
Or is it love returning

through an unfamiliar door,
the ones we overlooked
who loved us most?

And now I see
I have to let you go.
Waking as dawn commences

on the cold and empty street
I learn at last what others know:
persistence makes a ghost.

The Other

Who am I looking for
in this strange town –
its haunted squares
and alleyways, its unlit
gantries sloping down
past disused workings

to the sea? Too smart
to be my double,
too cautious for a friend,
he leaves a secret
trail for me to find:
a smear of beer stains

on the table top,
a trace of heartbreak
in the barmaid's eye.
In the time it takes
to down a pint,
scan the empty pool room

for a sign or look out
on the harbour lights
disintegrating into rain,
whatever drew me to this place
touches almost,
then comes clear.

I sense it is my father
leads me on – without reason,
without rest – down monumental
corridors of stone:
the happy-go-lucky only son,
discontented, dispossessed.

New England Afternoon

Blue shadows in the snow,
a frozen stream, a stricken pine
extending one bare arm
across the wilderness
that lies between my window
and the neighbouring farm,
the road to Boston
last night's blizzard closed,
a lone coyote howling
at the timberline – and me
remembering why I came
into this shifting landscape
sharp with light: a cornice
suspended, waiting to invade
the still day with its fall.
Up there, on Constitution Hill
where all the Union dead
are stored a priest looks out
from his clapboard house
at what the whiteness has redeemed,
tries hard but cannot bless it.
For the couple who have chosen this
until the day they die,
who sometimes holler, sometimes wave,
and stack their logs up high
against the cabin door,
this is the one experiment
in life that hasn't failed.
A month out here
has taught me what it's like
to long for their dream
and still not make it real,
to ache for the world
and not possess it.

The Great Divide

She looked at me and saw the bitter streets
    where I was born, the valley floor that offered
    no escape, the Chartist cobbles hard rain
glistened on, and everywhere a sense of failing light

streaking the uplands, making a theatre of them
    as it did – the unrelenting grimness of the north,
    its chapels, pit-heads, slag heaps, union halls,
processions through the darkness, millstone grit,

one great red furnace blazing from the Humber
    to the Sheaf – fought over, misbegotten, stratified.
    She looked straight through me to my father's eyes
black-rimmed and smiling after a long shift.

And as she gazed across the great divide,
    I let the balance of the landscape strain and give
    as if the world itself were undermined
and felt, not pity at the thought of it, but anger first, then pride.

The Western Sea

The day will come when those far hills
will make their presence felt.
You'll turn to me as you do now
and point across the bay,
interpreting a region I don't know.

These are the limits of the western sea,
its craggy outcrops stepping down,
intransigent and white with snow.

My once and future lover, now a friend,
look up into my looking down,
discern through misted windows
where your hand has cleared a space
the sureness of things coming to an end.

Encounter at the Well

They gave him huge impassive wings,
gold lashes and a flowering rod.
I spilled the water as he came to me.
And though they said I felt the breath of god
the urgency of man was in his voice.

He held me firmly from behind.
What I remember are his eyes,
unblinking though bright sunlight pierced the day,
a stiff breeze rushing through an upper room,
the yellow streak of pollen on my thighs.

The Girl Opens a Window and the Darkness is Postponed

A summer night. I sit outside,
aware of all the possibilities.

The girl opens a window
and the darkness is postponed.

I feel it holding back
above the town, above the rigid

branches of the trees.
Her hair cascades

against a red brick wall
as if the right word had been said.

Time changes what we are
to what we were: it happens

in an instant as she stoops
to lift the latch, lets in the season

or what's left of it,
the light escaping after her.

There's nothing I can offer
but this thing made out of words;

and the girl – who is potential –
shuts the window and it fades.

I'm learning what it means
to watch night fall.

A Last Love Poem

I was thinking how the daylight disappears,
how one thing blends into another thing
as over river, rooftops, silent park
time slips away without our noticing:
the wave collapses and a cold wind veers
through all the public places where we loved.

That's what it feels like these years on:
you were quite unexpected, and it seems
I've used up all the images I know –
midnight stations, coastal roads,
red wine, high windows, lace and sudden snow.
Don't be surprised if language fails me now.
I turn to face the sunlight. Let it go.

Jazz Train

Empty now but for the band,
    it makes its way past platforms
left deserted in the rain –
    through tunnels, sidings, cuttings
and lost villages like these
    where all we hear are notes
and undertones, shrill pleadings

from the trumpet
    or the solo saxophone,
the rhythm section going mad,
    a faded vocalist who swings
with one white orchid
    pinned behind her ear.
Pale ghosts climb down

from pit-heads and applaud.
    The passengers have left them,
gone back home, remembering
    only this and nights
like this. She might wake up
    and take him by the hand;
he might turn over in his sleep.

The band is rattling
    through the haunted towns,
searching for a way to make it start –
    to get between the dreamer
and the dream; a blue note
    humming down the miles of track,
a new republic of the heart.

Lavernock

There's a moment of pure stillness
between one wave and the next
when the silence in the heart is amplified.
It must have been an interval
like this – a pause in the heaving

of the stacked and waiting tide –
when the first words were transmitted
from a station near this point,
then sent out to the island,
skimming waves across the sound.

I loved it but I had to leave behind
the chapel with its green, sea-tarnished bell
and take the path that leads you down
between sparse dune-grass and a broken fence,
then brings you out and under

the horizon's curving rim
to meet with someone's double
where the cliffs disintegrate.
What did he give me as I halted there
to rifle through the shingle

for a blue-veined souvenir?
What can a stranger give you
on a stretch of empty shore
when you've been rendered silent
by the fullness of it all

unless he says, before you have the chance,
the selfsame things you might have said
about the exact colour of the sand –
if the words you'd been given
had fallen right – or how the tide

had gathered up its weight
to make one final push against the land
which lies subdued and waiting
for the surge it can't resist;
then turns like a soldier on his heel

to scale the rampart for a final look
and time begins again? I feared
the chapel and its rusted cross
had sunk into the headland
and were gone, that the others who'd come with me

who'd stood waiting on the brink
had driven from the cliff-top, also gone.
I scrambled up into the fading light.
The distant ridge came clear.
What he gave me was permission to go on.

Index of Titles and First Lines

A Note About the Author

Ian Parks was born in 1959 in Mexborough, Yorkshire. He was writer-in-residence at North Riding College during 1986-88 and received a Hawthornden Fellowship in 1991 and a Travelling Fellowship to the USA in 1994. One of the National Poetry Society New Poets in 1996, his first collection, *A Climb Through Altered Landscapes*, was published in 1998. He teaches creative writing at Leeds University and serves on the judging panel for the TMA theatre awards.

Other Books from Waywiser

Al Alvarez, *New & Selected Poems*
Peter Dale, *One Another*
B.H. Fairchild, *The Art of the Lathe*
Jeffrey Harrison, *The Names of Things: New & Selected Poems*
Joseph Harrison, *Someone Else's Name*
Anthony Hecht, *Collected Later Poems*
Anthony Hecht, *The Darkness and the Light*
Eric McHenry, *Potscrubber Lullabies*
Timothy Murphy, *Very Far North*
Daniel Rifenburgh, *Advent*
Mark Strand, *Blizzard of One**
Deborah Warren, *The Size of Happiness*
Clive Watkins, *Jigsaw*
Richard Wilbur, *Mayflies**
Richard Wilbur, *Collected Poems 1943-2004*
Norman Williams, *One Unblinking Eye*

FICTION

Gregory Heath, *The Entire Animal*
Matthew Yorke, *Chancing It*

NON-FICTION

Neil Berry, *Articles of Faith: The Story of British Intellectual Journalism*
Mark Ford, *A Driftwood Altar: Essays and Reviews*
Richard Wollheim, *Germs: A Memoir of Childhood*

*Expanded UK edition